WALKING *with* JESUS

Devotions for
Lent and Easter 2024

WALKING *with* JESUS

Devotions for Lent and Easter 2024

Editors of *Mornings with Jesus*

A GUIDEPOSTS DEVOTIONAL

Walking with Jesus: Devotions for Lent and Easter 2024

Published by Guideposts, 100 Reserve Road, Suite E200, Danbury, CT 06810
Guideposts.org

ACKNOWLEDGMENTS

Every attempt has been made to credit the sources of copyrighted material used in this book. If any such acknowledgment has been inadvertently omitted or miscredited, receipt of such information would be appreciated.

Cover design by Pamela Walker, W Design Studio
Interior design by Pamela Walker, W Design Studio
Cover photo by Dreamstime
Typeset by Aptara, Inc.

ISBN 978-1-961126-66-4 (softcover)
ISBN 978-1-961126-67-1 (epub)

Printed and bound in the United States of America

Even the darkest moments of the liturgy
are filled with joy, and Ash Wednesday,
the beginning of the Lenten fast,
is a day of happiness, a Christian Feast.

FATHER THOMAS MERTON

Low in the grave he lay, Jesus my Savior,
waiting the coming day, Jesus my Lord!

Up from the grave he arose;
with a mighty triumph o'er his foes;
he arose a victor from the dark domain,
and he lives forever, with his saints to reign.
He arose! He arose! Hallelujah! Christ arose!

Vainly they watch his bed, Jesus my Savior,
Vainly they seal the dead, Jesus my Lord!

Up from the grave he arose;
with a mighty triumph o'er his foes;
he arose a victor from the dark domain,
and he lives forever, with his saints to reign.
He arose! He arose! Hallelujah! Christ arose!

Death cannot keep its pretty, Jesus my Savior;
he tore the bars away, Jesus my Lord!

Up from the grave he arose;
with a mighty triumph o'er his foes;
he arose a victor from the dark domain,
and he lives forever, with his saints to reign.
He arose! He arose! Hallelujah! Christ arose!

"Christ Arose," Robert Lowry

INTRODUCTION

What does Lent mean to you? Is it all about sacrifice and self-denial? A penitential road to Easter's joyous Resurrection? It's certainly easy to argue that today's world of instant gratification has made Lent more of a hard sell.

And yet Lent offers us Christians an incomparable gift: a means of walking alongside Christ. As a time of praying, fasting, and giving alms, Lent gives us the ability to draw closer to the Redeemer who died for us by emulating His living example here on earth. What a privilege to become the people He intends us to be! *Walking with Jesus: Devotions for Lent and Easter* is a tender reminder that Jesus's Crucifixion, though brutal and merciless, offers all of us a new beginning full of forgiveness, purpose, and joy.

Like Advent, Lent is never mentioned in the Bible, though its roots are deeply biblical. Stretching from Ash Wednesday through Holy Week, Lent draws from Jesus's 40 days in the wilderness. (Are you wondering about those extra days on the calendar beyond 40? Sundays are meant for celebrating the Resurrection, no matter the season, and are exempt from our Lenten intentions and restrictions.) Jesus had been guided by the Spirit to the remote location, where, alone and fasting, He battled not only Satan's sinful offers but also the very human and perilous conditions of hunger and loneliness (Matthew 4:1–11).

Still, Christ's trek in the wilderness would be a fortifying, formative experience. Only afterward would Jesus gather His disciples and begin His ministry and miracles. As one of His followers later wrote, "You know that the testing of your faith produces perseverance" (James 1:3, NIV).

Lent derives from an Old English word for "spring," i.e., the time of year when days are lengthening. Appropriately, the colors of Lent often mirror the colors of spring. The vibrant greens, yellows, blues, purples, and reds—the last two common in liturgical garb—evoke the season's bursting into flower after a dormant winter, as we are called to blossom into better followers of Christ.

To do that, Lent challenges us to commit ourselves to the following practices:

Pray. The Parable of the Persistent Widow (Luke 18) teaches us that God answers the faithful. In fact, prayer was a staple of Jesus's earthly life all the way through the Crucifixion. By focusing our attention and praise on God and by reading Scripture, we seek to grow closer to Him and be transformed by the encounter. As Paul once counseled, "Be joyful in hope, patient in affliction, faithful in prayer" (Romans 12:12, NIV).

Fast. Forgoing food and comforts is a theme dating to the Old Testament. Fasting purifies the self and separates us very deliberately from earthly distractions. As Acts tells us, such self-control also earns divine notice: "While they were worshiping the Lord and fasting, the Holy Spirit said, 'Set apart for me Barnabas and Saul for the work to which I have called them'" (Acts 13:2, NIV).

Give. God's constant care for the impoverished is a refrain throughout the Bible, including His laws to Moses on gleaning (Leviticus 19:9). Our chosen Lenten sacrifices enable us to look with fresh compassion on others whose sufferings are not by choice; by showing charity and mercy to others, we draw closer to Jesus's holy example and please God. We may not have the ability to multiply loaves of bread and fish, but we can witness and ease the burden of a fellow child of God, as we have been instructed to do: "Whoever oppresses the poor shows contempt for their Maker, but whoever is kind to the needy honors God" (Proverbs 14:31, NIV).

As Lent comes to an end, Holy Week begins. Over the course of one tempestuous week, Jesus would experience, as the Gospels show, the highest of highs and the lowest of lows. Palm Sunday would see Jesus triumphantly welcomed to Jerusalem with hosannas and palm branches (John 12:12–13). Yet days later, on Holy Thursday, He would be sold into imprisonment by Judas and denied three times by Simon Peter (Matthew 27, John 18). By Good Friday's end, He would be tortured, mocked, and crucified, His body entombed in a borrowed grave (John 19). And yet, two days later, Jesus's followers would find His body gone from the tomb and then interact with angels and the risen Christ Himself

(John 20). Out of His great love for us, imperfect as we are, He sacrificed Himself and was Resurrected. What a glorious example for all of us!

Within *Walking with Jesus: Devotions for Lent and Easter*, you'll find daily devotions—personal stories with spiritual resonance—that mirror and examine a Lenten theme, carrying through God's lessons in a modern world. Devotionals have become increasingly popular for a reason: Reading them is a manifestation of our desire to know God and understand His expectations and tasks for us, a longing that supersedes even the needs of our bodies.

Jesus answered, "It is written: 'Man shall not live on bread alone, but on every word that comes from the mouth of God.'"

—MATTHEW 4:4 (NIV)

You may already know the beloved publication *Mornings with Jesus*. The devotions here, curated from those pages, were written by women of faith from every walk of life, and their unique perspectives on how Lent resonates in their life will invite you to contemplate and redirect the course of your own faith life. Consider reading this devotional with family members and friends to discuss your interpretations. Even if you do not have a daily devotional reading habit, Lent is a powerful time to incorporate devotions into your worship practice.

Lent offers us so much more than an opportunity to give up chocolate, gossip, or wine. Through the choices we make—by praying, fasting, and giving to others—we can enrich our faith and strengthen our relationship with Christ. It is simple really: "Humble yourselves, therefore, under God's mighty hand, that he may lift you up in due time" (1 Peter 5:6, NIV).

Lisa Guernsey

ASH WEDNESDAY, FEBRUARY 14

To console those who mourn in Zion, to give them beauty for ashes, the oil of joy for mourning, the garment of praise for the spirit of heaviness....

ISAIAH 61:3 (NKJV)

In the Old Testament, people expressed sorrow and repentance by dressing in sackcloth and ashes. After Job lost almost everything he had, he was confused about the nature of God. He said, "I take back everything I said, and I sit in dust and ashes to show my repentance" (Job 42:6, NLT).

Upon hearing that the Jewish people were about to be eradicated, Mordecai—Esther's cousin—mourned with sackcloth and ashes (Esther 4:1). But it was Jesus who challenged all with His words: "Unless you repent you will all...perish" (Luke 13:5, NKJV).

The tradition of Ash Wednesday can symbolically remind us of Jesus's sacrifice at Easter. Some believers wear the symbol of the cross in ashes on their foreheads. Others simply begin a season of sacrificing something in their lives to show their repentance.

Repentance is a teaching I've embraced and understood ever since I first gave my heart to Jesus as a child. As I've grown older, I've come to understand an enlarged view of the symbolism of ashes. It takes my breath away, just thinking about it.

Isaiah prophesied Jesus would bring beauty for ashes, joy for mourning, and garments of praise through His death, Resurrection, and second coming. When we repent and believe in the promises of God, Jesus gives us the beauty of His complete forgiveness, now and forever. Our sins lie in ashes, with no more power to overcome us. Tears of sadness—for cheers of gladness. What a beautiful exchange!

REBECCA BARLOW JORDAN

FAITH STEP

Confess any sinful habits that may have crept into your life. Then thank Jesus for taking the ashes of your sin in exchange for the beauty of His forgiveness.

THURSDAY, FEBRUARY 15

No, I tell you, but unless you change your hearts and lives, you will die just as they did.

LUKE 13:3 (CEB)

My middle son was quick to seek forgiveness when he did something wrong. In that respect he fit the mold of a middle-child personality wanting to make things right between us as soon as possible.

But he was a child. And human. So he had plenty of opportunities to put that into practice.

On one particularly "Mommy's had enough" day, he came to me with his traditional "I'm sorry" for a familiar infraction. Without thinking of the consequences the words would have as they resonated in my own soul, I said, "Honey, if you were really sorry, you wouldn't do it again."

That was the day I understood the true meaning of repentance. It's not a word on a billboard. Not a ritual at the beginning of Lent. Not a puppy's tail between his legs, head-hanging-low heart response for our mess-ups.

Repentance, as Jesus described it, is a change of heart. It's honoring what Jesus wants more than the pull of a temptation, changing our way of thinking about what we're entitled to, what we deserve, if that runs contrary to what the Bible teaches. It's a transformation from one way of thinking—one mindset—to another that is not only spiritually healthy but God-pleasing.

The ashes of Ash Wednesday represent repentance, a symbol of grief over our sins, sins that sent Jesus to the Cross. But commemorating grief stops short if it doesn't commemorate true repentance, the change of heart that marks us for life.

My son had a vast reservoir of "I'm sorry's." The day eventually came when he didn't need them so often. He'd had a change of heart.

CYNTHIA RUCHTI

FAITH STEP

At the beginning of the 40 days of Lent, purchase a charcoal or gray notebook (or re-cover another notebook with gray or charcoal cloth or paper) and record the ways you've had a change of heart in how you think about yourself, others, and Jesus.

FRIDAY, FEBRUARY 16

For we died and were buried with Christ by baptism. And just as Christ was raised from the dead by the glorious power of the Father, now we also may live new lives.

ROMANS 6:4 (NLT)

My neighbor's weeping willow slouches, with ominous melancholy, toward our back fence. Its branches do just that—weep—onto our yard: twigs and small, slender, tear-shaped leaves. It invades the airspace of my backyard, and has, on windy days, dropped large branches, oblivious to the nuisance and danger it creates. All right, it does provide shade for the house, which is sometimes appreciated. But as the weather cools and the leaves drop in earnest, I'm not so appreciative.

One branch in particular annoys me—completely dead, leafless, the gray pallor of its skeletal limbs, which are like finger bones reaching for the sky. It waits for the next storm to crash into my back deck, but until then does nothing, serves nothing. Provides no shade and disrupts the otherwise lovely view.

This morning, washing dishes, I looked out at the branch, my eye pulled by a flash of red against the gray. A woodpecker clung to the underside of the branch, its bright red-capped head drawing my attention. It pecked at the wood, apparently finding food within. Then a pair of cardinals flitted among the branches, stopping on the smooth, dead branch to offer a trilling song.

What appears useless or annoying is not always so. Sometimes the starkness allows a better view of the beauty we would otherwise miss.

Jesus let go of His privilege and power, and actually died for us, in order to bring us life. Following Jesus requires us to also let go of our ambitions and die to ourselves, so that we can live new lives.

KERI WYATT KENT

FAITH STEP

What annoying or useless thing in your life might actually serve a purpose, even if that purpose is to provide a backdrop to the beauty you might not otherwise see?

SATURDAY, FEBRUARY 17

After the sabbath, as the first day of the week was dawning, Mary Magdalene and the other Mary went to see the tomb. And suddenly there was a great earthquake; for an angel of the Lord, descending from heaven, came and rolled back the stone and sat on it. His appearance was like lightning, and his clothing white as snow. For fear of him the guards shook and became like dead men.

MATTHEW 28:1–4 (NRSVUE)

EVERY YEAR, AS LENT BEGINS, I wonder if Easter will really "happen" for me again this year. And every year, I am surprised that Holy Week can feel new and real. There is always more of me that can wake up to the dawn of Christ's Resurrection.

Finding these new places in myself that need resurrection rests in the fact that I can always relate to the guards in this story. They are the ones who have been placed there to guard Jesus's body. They are the ones who experience

His Resurrection as a great earthquake. They are the ones who shake and become like dead men in the presence of the angel at the empty tomb.

There is always some part of my own faith life that relates to the guards. Some part of me that has become comfortable with protecting authority—whether it's the authority of the institutions I put my trust in or my own. And then sometime during Lent and Holy Week, something happens to challenge that comfort and to show me the empty nature of it all. It usually feels like an earthquake, a disruption that terrifies my defenses. During this sacred week, I am given the grace to let this part of me—this "guard," this defensive posture—be shaken off in the presence of the angel of the Lord.

ELIZABETH BERNE DeGEAR

FAITH STEP

Assess your faith life. Which parts guard beliefs or practices that are no longer genuinely alive for you? Try shaking them off to make room for some new aspect of Christ to enter your life, even if it feels like an earthquake or a bolt of lightning.

SUNDAY, FEBRUARY 18

Again he said, "What shall we say the kingdom of God is like, or what parable shall we use to describe it? It is like a mustard seed, which is the smallest seed you plant in the ground. Yet when planted, it grows and becomes the largest of all garden plants, with such big branches that the birds of the air can perch in its shade."

MARK 4:30–32 (NIV)

MY BACKYARD IS LOOKING a little sparse these days. The rosebushes are squat and trimmed back, and the hydrangea bushes look like a clump of twigs. The Japanese maples have yet to bloom. Even the lemon tree looks forlorn.

But I know that the beauty is coming. Spring is just around the corner. Soon the rosebush will be sprouting leaves and the maple will fill out with its vibrant greenery. It happens every year.

It is so easy to think that things are what they seem. That things will stay the same. But Jesus sees things differently.

Taking the tiniest seed possible, the mustard seed, He says, "The smallest seed will become the largest plant."

This is how things work when it comes to Jesus. He turns everything on its ear. The blind shall see. The lame shall walk. The least significant will become the most significant. The first will be last, and the last will be first. This should give us great hope. As His truth takes root in our hearts, we have no idea how large His kingdom can grow within us. How His love will change us. How His mercy will shape our lives and give shelter to those around us.

He will grow us and form us into more than we can ever hope or imagine. He takes small, unruly lives and makes them large and lovely. Just take it from the mustard seed.

SUSANNA FOTH AUGHTMON

FAITH STEP

Plant a seedling in a cup by your window. Check out its progress each morning. As you watch the seedling, remind yourself that Jesus is growing His Kingdom in you.

MONDAY, FEBRUARY 19

Don't let your hearts be troubled.
Trust in God, and trust also in me.

JOHN 14:1 (NLT)

IT'S HARD TO IMAGINE HOW confused and troubled the disciples must have felt. They had witnessed the crowds adoring Jesus as He rode into Jerusalem on a donkey. They had heard people hailing Him as King of Israel. But then, as the twelve disciples celebrated the Passover meal with Jesus, the mood abruptly switched. Jesus predicted that one of them would betray Him.

He said that Peter would deny knowing Him and they would all desert Him. Jesus even said that He would be going away—that He would soon die. His words made no sense to them.

There are times when I feel confused and troubled. Maybe it's a phone call or a message relaying bad news. Or some strange turn of events that makes no sense at all. Or even the cumulative effect of repeated disappointments and failures.

Just as a child who is hurt or scared runs to a parent to be held and hear soothing words spoken in their ear, I need to know where to turn. During that Passover meal, Jesus spoke comforting words to calm His disciples' hearts: "Don't let your hearts be troubled…trust in Me." Those words are also spoken for me.

Jesus knows exactly what troubles my heart and He knows the words I need to hear. But I have to trust Him enough to go to Him with my need and then listen to His voice. He may speak to me through a stirring in my spirit or by a strong sense of His abiding presence. Or He may lead me to a passage of Scripture that addresses my situation and brings encouragement and comfort to my hurting heart. Either way, I can depend on Jesus to speak soothing words when I need them.

DIANNE NEAL MATTHEWS

FAITH STEP

Do you need to hear comforting words from Jesus today? Ask Him to speak to your troubled heart, either through His Spirit within you or through the written Word.

TUESDAY, FEBRUARY 20

When the soldiers crucified Jesus, they took his clothes, dividing them into four shares, one for each of them, with the undergarment remaining.

JOHN 19:23 (NIV)

FOR SEVERAL YEARS, A CHURCH in our town presented a massive production that included hyperrealistic scenes depicting issues teenagers and adults face, such as the consequences of drug use, drinking and driving, suicide, relationship collapse, and disinterest in the Gospel.

This year during the Easter season, I thought about the volunteers who were part of the most heart-gripping scene—the Crucifixion of Jesus. The church had no trouble getting volunteers to play the part of the grieving mother of Jesus. Hands went up to volunteer to play the part of Mary Magdalene. The part of John, the disciple Jesus loved, was an easy role to fill. Few said, "Hey, sign me up to play Jesus. I want to be the one to wear a crown of thorns, hang for hours on a splinter-ridden cross, be mocked, spit upon, held up to ridicule. Sign me up to be bound to that cross."

Jesus had no discussion with His Father that included "Could I be John instead of Me? How about one of the soldiers? I like their uniforms." Instead, He voluntarily laid down His life for what we needed most—forgiveness of our sins. It's no cliché to say He died so we could live.

I can put myself in the scene at the foot of the cross. But I can't fully imagine it from His viewpoint because that part could only be played in real life—real Life—by Him.

CYNTHIA RUCHTI

FAITH STEP

Consider celebrating the impact of the Crucifixion through the eyes of each of the people we're told were nearby. Imagine their emotions and responses, then compare them to the intensity of your response to Christ's sacrifice.

WEDNESDAY, FEBRUARY 21

He must increase, but I must decrease.

JOHN 3:30 (ESV)

When my husband and I planned a trip to northern California several years ago, we looked forward to stopping at the Redwood National Park, "home of the tallest trees on Earth." We did a little reading ahead of time about the redwood trees' size (as tall as 360 feet!) and their life span (up to 2,000 years!). We marveled at the online pictures of the three "Drive-Through" trees located on the coast.

All this information did not prepare us for the actual sight of the giant redwoods. Surrounded by the huge trunks, I craned my neck to try to see the tops soaring toward the heavens. I almost toppled over backward. The sheer majesty of the redwoods made me feel like a little bug on the forest floor.

It's not always a bad thing to feel small. Some of John the Baptist's disciples complained that everybody had started flocking to Jesus instead of to them. Rather than feel disgruntled, John was happy to hear of Jesus's growing popularity. That meant he had done his job of preparing people's hearts to receive the Messiah. Now that Jesus had come, John would gladly decrease in importance.

Feeling insignificant can help us more fully appreciate the majesty of Jesus. It can flood us with a sense of wonder that Jesus considered us worth dying for despite our sins, shortcomings, and frailties. An awareness of our weakness sets the stage for Him to display His strength and power in our life. That's important because our goal is to point people to Jesus, not shine the light on our own talents and achievements. Once we become willing to decrease in importance, then the evidence of Him in our life will become greater. We will have done our job of pointing others to the Messiah.

DIANNE NEAL MATTHEWS

FAITH STEP

The next time you're feeling small and insignificant, use it as an opportunity to magnify Jesus. List His qualities that sustain and empower you. Thank Him for surrounding your life with His greatness.

THURSDAY, FEBRUARY 22

As long as the earth exists, seedtime and harvest, cold and hot, summer and autumn, day and night will not cease.

GENESIS 8:22 (CEB)

THE DAY THE FIRST SEED catalog of the year arrived in the mail, it was twenty below zero with a biting wind chill. My first thought was, *That's just cruel.* Pulling my wool sweater tighter around me, I stared out at the snow-covered ground, the garden stiff and lifeless. The seed catalog cover made me sigh. It would be many months before I'd see color like that in my garden. This was the season of hibernation, not the season of growth. Too many gray days made me resistant to the joy potential the seed catalog held.

"Plant a future seed." The idea came as soft as a summer breeze. Instead of mourning the contrast between my current circumstances and what the catalog promised, I could plant a virtual seed.

I spent the next hour plotting what new flowers I'd add to my garden in the spring. What would my vegetable raised beds hold? A new variety of an old favorite? Should I try cabbages again and find a more efficient way to fight off the cabbage-loving chipmunks?

My view out the window showed the same bitter, stark, cold whiteness. The view in my heart sported all kinds of anticipated color, dewy, sun-drenched magenta blossoms and fragrant herbs.

Jesus knew we'd be prone to getting mentally stuck in our current circumstances without a nudge from Him to think ahead to the joys that lie before us. The spring at the end of the winter. The lush garden of answers to replace our barren seasons. The heaven that awaits.

Winter to spring. Illness to health. Stress to peace. Broken to mended. It might be time for me to plant a few more seeds.

CYNTHIA RUCHTI

FAITH STEP

Have you planted seeds, mapped out a garden, envisioned what it will be like when this season of life passes? When the medical crisis abates? When the prodigal comes home? When you make it through financial upheaval? Plant a faith seed today.

FRIDAY, FEBRUARY 23

Blessed are the meek: for they shall inherit the earth.

MATTHEW 5:5 (KJV)

In what we call "The Sermon on the Mount," Jesus outlines some of the traits He wants His followers to display. One of them, possibly the most difficult and most representative of His own character, is meekness.

I often hear people misunderstand the definition of meekness, describing it as shyness or quietness, not wanting to ruffle any feathers. It seems so many Christians embrace a definition like this, believing it's a sin to ever offend anyone else by speaking up or saying no to a request. Nothing could be further from the truth of Jesus's teaching.

What He meant by meekness, what He Himself embodied, was self-control in the face of adversity. Gentleness. It's the idea of wild horses that have been tamed. We see this time and time again in the New Testament, but never more than when He is on the Cross. Imagine the restraint Jesus had to show in order to fulfill His mission. He could have come down unscathed; He could have obliterated His enemies. But He chose obedience. He chose love.

Meekness does not seem to have much value in today's world. With credit cards, fast food, and social media, people seem more willing than ever to throw off any sense of self-restraint. If I want it, I can buy it. If I'm hungry, I can eat within minutes. And on social media, I can tell my story to an international audience. We often suffer from consequences we never took the time to consider because we aren't meek. But we need to be if we want to be blessed.

GWEN FORD FAULKENBERRY

FAITH STEP

Consider the wild horses in your life that need taming. Don't make a purchase, send a text, or write a Facebook post today unless you can do it in the name of Jesus. See what blessing a little meekness brings!

SATURDAY, FEBRUARY 24

Jesus said, "Father, forgive them, for they do not know what they are doing."

LUKE 23:34 (NIV)

DURING THE LENTEN SEASON, followers of Jesus through the centuries have taken time to ponder the "Seven Last Words" of Christ on the Cross.

In the moments where He was fulfilling His promise to bring salvation to all humankind, each sentence He spoke echoes with the music of love, grace, and compassion.

Because of the gift of Scripture, we can join those who stood beneath the Cross and hear His voice as He continues to speak to us today. The first recorded words are a prayer, very fitting for the Son who spent so much time in communion with the Father. Yet the prayer is no longer "Remove this cup," or even "Give me strength to endure." He intercedes for the very soldiers who pounded nails into Him, for the jeering crowd who had screamed, "Crucify Him," and even the men who scrabbled around in the shadow of the

Cross, ignoring His suffering and greedily grasping for His few possessions.

Suffering in our life comes in many forms. Sometimes others are intentionally cruel. We may face injustice, attacks, or betrayals that affect our work or our relationships. We may be harmed by crime, war, poverty. Other times the wounds are less deliberate. The deepest pain sometimes comes through a thoughtless statement from a child or spouse or a careless act by a dear friend. When others hurt us, let us fight through the pain and tears to grasp this prayer of mercy: "Father, forgive."

SHARON HINCK

FAITH STEP

Who has hurt you recently? Ask Jesus to help you pray this prayer of mercy for them.

SUNDAY, FEBRUARY 25

We love each other because he loved us first.

1 JOHN 4:19 (NLT)

THE OTHER NIGHT MY YOUNGEST SON, Addison, and I were lying on the couch watching TV. This is becoming difficult since he is 10 years old and already 5 feet tall. I am snuggling a small adult. He still lets me kiss him every once in a while, even though he is so big. With his arm wrapped around my neck, I looked at him and said, "Addie, how much do you love me?" He said, "A lot." And I said, "How much is a lot?" He said, "You and Dad are under God. Then comes Flash. Then my brothers. Then my friends." Then he turned back to watch the show.

It is a good thing to be loved more than the dog. That is high praise. But I especially love that Addie knows the One who loves him most of all. He knows that my husband, Scott, and I love him to death. But Jesus? Jesus's love gives Addison a chance at new life.

Jesus surrounds us on every side, never leaving us for a moment. Even when we can't feel Him. Even when life is difficult or even tragic. Even when we are questioning and doubting. His love is ever present. Tethering us to His goodness and His grace. It is so huge, we can't fathom it. There are moments when we catch a small glimpse of the greatness of Jesus's love. The knowledge that He gave everything so that we could have a relationship with Him. The understanding that without His love we have nothing. With it we have all that we'll ever need. It leaves us breathless. All we can do is try to love Him back with everything that is within us. Because He loved us first.

SUSANNA FOTH AUGHTMON

FAITH STEP

Draw a heart on a piece of paper. Fill the heart with five distinct ways that Jesus shows you His love.

MONDAY, FEBRUARY 26

You intended to harm me, but God intended it for good to accomplish what is now being done, the saving of many lives.

GENESIS 50:20 (NIV)

JOSEPH'S BROTHERS HAD ABUSED HIM and sold him to slave traders years earlier. Now they found themselves at his mercy, the second most powerful man in Egypt. No wonder they quaked with the fear that Joseph might take revenge. But Joseph assured them of his care and protection. He explained that although they had meant to harm him, God brought great good out of their evil intentions. The brothers' actions had brought Joseph to his present position, where his leadership saved many lives during the long famine.

The Old Testament includes other instances of God bringing good out of evil. The supreme example, however, is found in the New Testament's Easter story. The anger, hatred, and brutality that led men to crucify Jesus. The pain and suffering He endured that day. The confusion and horror His followers felt after His death. All of these things paved the way for His Resurrection a few days later, when God's plan was fully revealed. The very actions used by Christ's enemies to stop His ministry and destroy Him actually fulfilled His mission: to sacrifice His life as payment for the sin of anyone who chooses to believe in Him.

If God brought the greatest good for the human race out of the worst evil ever committed, surely I can trust Him to do the same in my personal life. Romans 8:28 promises that God is working everything out for the good of those who love Him. I find comfort knowing He can overrule every wrong committed against me and turn it for His own purposes.

And every year the Easter story reminds me that God's goodness can overcome any evil.

DIANNE NEAL MATTHEWS

FAITH STEP

Think about the most hurtful thing you've recently experienced. Ask Jesus to use this situation to accomplish His good purposes in the lives of everyone involved.

TUESDAY, FEBRUARY 27

He cuts off every branch of mine that doesn't produce fruit, and he prunes the branches that do bear fruit so they will produce even more.

JOHN 15:2 (NLT)

For nearly a decade, our family lived on a yard bordered by a fence on which grapevines grew. The yard also held a peach tree, a plum tree, two apple trees, and about two dozen raspberry bushes.

I'm no horticulturalist, so I asked the former residents to teach me how to care for these plants so they'd produce fruit. Following their instructions, my husband and I brought out the pruning shears every spring and set to work. We snipped and cut vines and branches until it seemed unlikely they'd ever grow back.

The art of pruning seemed a bit harsh to us, but it was obviously effective because the plants always gifted us with a luscious harvest. I canned fruit, preserved jams and jellies, made juice, and baked pies. And still there was plenty of fresh produce to share with friends.

At times in my life I've felt as though Jesus has pruned me, and His use of the shears has seemed a bit harsh. He's lopped off pride, procrastination, greed, and even gluttony by allowing me to experience loneliness, physical pain, prickly interpersonal relationships, and financial uncertainty. His labors have taught me humility, gratitude, and self-discipline. Ultimately my faith journey has deepened, and I'm more in love with Him today than ever before.

Jesus's method of helping us flourish really works. The process is painful at times, and we might be tempted to question His care and wisdom. But let's rest in His work, knowing that His desire is to produce in us a harvest of righteousness.

GRACE FOX

FAITH STEP

Eat a piece of your favorite fruit. As you do, thank Jesus for loving you enough to prune you so your life will produce a rich harvest.

WEDNESDAY, FEBRUARY 28

Jesus said to his disciples, "All who want to come after me must say no to themselves, take up their cross, and follow me."

MATTHEW 16:24 (CEB)

WHAT AN INTERESTING CONVERSATION THIS must have been between Jesus and His disciples. This was the first time Jesus let people know He was going to suffer, be killed, and rise again on the third day. His disciples rebelled against the idea, not understanding that it all had to happen in order for any of us to be redeemed.

After chiding Peter for listening to human instincts instead of the will of God, Jesus told His followers that all who want to come after Him would have to say no to themselves (their human instincts and desires), take up their cross, and follow Him.

"Whoa. Slow down there, Jesus. Our crosses? This is not what we signed up for." Those words aren't recorded in Scripture, but somebody must have been thinking them.

When life gets tough, are you tempted to say, "This is not what I signed up for!"? But it is. To follow Jesus means walking the rocky, painful paths He walked, if that's what's ahead.

Jesus didn't tell us to pick our crosses. He told us to pick up our crosses and follow Him. "Walk this way," in other words. Head high, despite the weight of that cross, eyes forward, getting up if we stumble, and faithfully obedient, grateful for His promise never to leave us or forsake us, every step of the way.

CYNTHIA RUCHTI

FAITH STEP

Memorize this related verse for times when you feel the weight of your cross pulling you downward: "For the Human One is about to come with the majesty of his Father with his angels. And then he will repay each one for what that person has done" (Matthew 16:27, CEB).

THURSDAY, FEBRUARY 29

Many are the plans in a person's heart,
but it is the LORD's purpose that prevails.

PROVERBS 19:21 (NIV)

ON A RECENT VISIT WITH our three-year-old granddaughter, we read the Bible story of Jesus's arrest in Gethsemane. She had many questions about why people wanted to hurt Jesus. Her father did a beautiful job sharing the Gospel with her. He also explained that the religious leaders wanted to keep control and were worried because people were following Jesus. He told her that Jesus allowed Himself to be hurt because He loves us so much. She listened with rapt attention. When he finished, she had one question: "Daddy, how do I get control?"

We laughed, but after she was tucked in bed, we discussed how her question epitomized the human condition. From the Garden of Eden until today, we are presented with the wonderful truth of Jesus's love, grace, and sacrifice on our behalf. Yet often our response is "I want to be the boss."

I'd like to think I'm more spiritually mature now that I'm no longer three, but the truth is I still often miss the point. I dictate to Jesus exactly how He should answer my prayers, but if He doesn't do things my way, doubt twists my thoughts into knots. I set a course for myself, but when I don't get what I want, selfish ambition coils in my heart. I grow impatient with Jesus's timing, frustrated with where He's placed me. Grasping for control causes me to lash out at the One who offers me peace.

In His tenderness, Jesus reminds me I'm not in control. When I trust His purposes, peace floods me. Then He amazes me as I catch glimpses of those purposes—far richer, deeper, and better than any of my plans.

SHARON HINCK

FAITH STEP

Memorize today's verse and ask Jesus to place your plans in His hands.

FRIDAY, MARCH 1

So he sent other servants to tell them, "The feast has been prepared. The bulls and fattened cattle have been killed, and everything is ready. Come to the banquet!"

MATTHEW 22:4 (NLT)

A FEW YEARS AGO, I GOT HOOKED on TV singing competition shows. I enjoy hearing the background stories of the contestants and seeing them step out in courage to pursue their dreams. Some of them are so talented and poised that they already seem like professionals, but I like seeing the ones who blossom before the viewers' eyes, thanks to their growing self-confidence and the expert coaching they receive.

The negative thing about these shows is the audition phase. It's tough to see some hopeful contestant sing her heart out and get no positive response. On one show, the judges' chairs are turned around with their backs to the singers. If judges like what they hear, they push a button. Then their chair turns around as a sign lights up saying "I Want You."

I'm so glad we don't have to approach God like that. He has already done all that's needed for me to become His adopted child. I don't have to audition for His love. I don't need to work as hard as I can to become good enough for His approval. Through His life, death, and Resurrection, Jesus made it possible for me to enter into a personal relationship with Him. He wants me just as I am.

Unlike television judges, Jesus doesn't have His back turned to us until we do something worthy of His attention. He pursues us with outstretched hands and love in His eyes, saying, "Come!" Once we answer His call and submit to His coaching, we will blossom before His eyes. And our life, while not perfect, will indeed be a banquet.

DIANNE NEAL MATTHEWS

FAITH STEP

Do you sometimes feel like you don't measure up, that you need to earn God's favor? Read Jeremiah 31:3, John 3:16, and Ephesians 2:8–9. Meditate on the unconditional love that Jesus demonstrated for you on the Cross.

SATURDAY, MARCH 2

For this very reason, Christ died and returned to life so that he might be the Lord of both the dead and the living.

ROMANS 14:9 (NIV)

I SAT AT THE TABLE, SPOONING JELLY BEANS into bright-colored plastic eggs and filling Easter baskets with chocolate bunnies. My gaze settled on the carton of dyed eggs. How difficult would today's hunt be? It all depended on who did the hiding.

I hide things well. Many of my secrets I keep locked away from others. Some I try—unsuccessfully—to keep hidden from myself. But I can't conceal anything from Jesus.

At the Crucifixion, Jesus absorbed every sin ever committed. To save the thieves hanging beside Him, Jesus took on their sins. For Judas, He bore the guilt of His own betrayer. For Martha, Mary's sister, He carried her critical nature. Murderer, drunk, blackmailer—the list is endless. The magnitude of His sacrifice overwhelms me. For One who'd never sinned, the burden must have been horrendous. But it hasn't diminished the pile of sins I've heaped at the base of the Cross.

He's borne the weight of all my sins as I stumble through life. He asks only that I repent and make Him my Lord. That's the beauty of the Resurrection. He uncovers the darkness we try to hide and exposes it to light. And through His blood we can throw off all our sins and become like Him.

What sin has Jesus helped you overcome? You can rest knowing He's risen far above the hate, hurts, and pain we've inflicted on one another—and on Him. He plays only one role now—Lord of lords and King of kings. He is risen!

HEIDI GAUL

FAITH STEP

Make a list of the sin-titles that you've worn in life, then tear it up and throw it away. On a clean sheet of paper, write "forgiven." Celebrate Easter as a child of the King.

SUNDAY, MARCH 3

The wine supply ran out during the festivities, so Jesus' mother told him, "They have no more wine." "Dear woman, that's not our problem," Jesus replied. "My time has not yet come."

JOHN 2:3–4 (NLT)

THERE IS A TIME FOR everything, a season for every activity under the heavens" (Ecclesiastes 3:1, NIV). Wise words, these are. So wise, in fact, that even Jesus applied them to His life. On several occasions when people urged Him to do things that would risk revealing His identity as the Messiah, He replied, "My time has not yet come." He knew His Father's redemptive plan and refused to rush ahead of it.

Hours before His death, Jesus spoke about time again. He said, "Now the time has come for the Son of Man to enter into his glory" (John 12:23, NIV). The wait was over, and He knew that His life's purpose was about to be fulfilled.

My husband worked as a civil engineer for 11 years, but his heart's desire was to work in career Christian camping. For several months we prayed about the possibility of making the switch, but we felt the answer was "Wait." His time had not yet come to leave his job. Nine more years passed. Nearly every day we prayed for wisdom to recognize when to take action. And then one day we knew.

Jesus knew the importance of timing in fulfilling His Father's purposes. As always, He's our example and our teacher. We can trust Him to show us whether to wait or move forward in whatever situation we face. When we're intent on following His lead, He'll be faithful to show us what to do.

GRACE FOX

FAITH STEP

Read Ecclesiastes 3:1–8. The first stanza says, "There is a time for everything." Replace the word *everything* with a personal application. Then thank Jesus for promising to show you when the time is right for those circumstances to be fulfilled.

MONDAY, MARCH 4

"[The Lord says] 'But for you who fear my name, the Sun of Righteousness will rise with healing in his wings.'"

MALACHI 4:2 (NLT)

WHAT KIND OF CRAZY VACATION *is this?* I wondered as I shut off the alarm at 2:30 a.m.! But the brochure listed "seeing the sun rise over Haleakala Crater" as one of the "Top Ten Things to Do on Maui." The hotel staff recommended that we leave at 3:15 to allow plenty of time to drive to the other side of the island. We followed the winding road to the top of the mountain, arriving more than an hour before sunrise. Time seemed to drag by as we sat in the car, waiting. Finally, we joined the crowd on the peak, eyes strained toward the east.

Shivering in the darkness, I couldn't help wondering, *Is a sunrise really worth all this trouble?* Then I thought about how Jesus's followers must have felt the day after His Crucifixion. They didn't know it at the time, but they were waiting for the Son to rise. Jesus had made comments about His Resurrection that they failed to understand. Their world seemed dark and confused. How could the Messiah have been executed—wasn't He supposed to break the Roman oppression and rule their nation? With their Master dead and buried, all they could do was wait.

Some days I struggle with some of the same feelings those early disciples had. A trial or crisis strikes suddenly and makes my world seem cold and dark. I feel confused about what's happening and wonder why Jesus seems to be absent from the situation. But even when I don't recognize His presence in my life, Jesus is there. And when He does visibly show up, I'll remember what I was about to learn that dark morning: waiting for the sun to rise over a mountain is always worth it.

DIANNE NEAL MATTHEWS

FAITH STEP

Is there a situation that makes you feel like you're in the dark, waiting for the Son to show up? Ask Him to help you sense His presence.

TUESDAY, MARCH 5

But one of his disciples, Judas Iscariot, who was later to betray him, objected, "Why wasn't this perfume sold and the money given to the poor? It was worth a year's wages." He did not say this because he cared about the poor but because he was a thief; as keeper of the money bag, he used to help himself to what was put into it.

JOHN 12:4–6 (NIV)

HAVE YOU EVER WONDERED HOW Judas—who lived and walked alongside Jesus for years—could betray His Lord and Savior? I found some clues in this account in the Gospel of John. On the surface, Judas might have appeared compassionate and concerned for the poor, but his underlying motive was selfish.

When I read this, I shook my head. My first thought was that if I had heard Jesus's words daily and walked in His presence, I would have resisted temptation. Then the Holy Spirit reminded me that I do walk in Jesus's presence, and

Scripture gives me His words, yet I also cave in to selfish motives.

Last week, I saw a glowing tribute posted for a project in which I'd been involved. The names of others who had participated were listed. My name was not. It stung. Recognition wasn't my conscious goal. I'd worked on the project to serve Jesus and to help others. Yet my reaction showed me how muddled my motives truly were.

Like Judas, it can be easy for us to present a face of best intentions, perhaps not even realizing how much our human desires are entangled in the choices we make.

I thanked Jesus for the painful glimpse into my own heart. I asked Him to forgive me and to live through me. He emptied Himself and took the form of a servant, and that's the sort of motivation I want to have.

SHARON HINCK

FAITH STEP

Ask Jesus to shine a light on any selfish motives lurking within your choices. Ask Him to give you His heart of genuine love.

WEDNESDAY, MARCH 6

For assuredly, I say to you, whoever says to this mountain, "Be removed and be cast into the sea," and does not doubt in his heart, but believes that those things he says will be done, he will have whatever he says.

MARK 11:23 (NKJV)

I ADMIRE THE GARDEN CULTURE in the suburban area in which I live. Life is blossoming all around. That's probably a reason why I love the theme of nature Jesus uses in the New Testament. He references nature and agriculture many times in His parables and messages to us—mountains, trees, vines, branches, fruit, soil, crops, seeds, and so on. When I first came to Christ, I took these verses at face value. Some were pretty straightforward, like planting seed in good soil (Mark 4:8) and the fact that He is the True Vine as we are the branches (John 15:5). Those make sense. But there are others that are harder to understand.

For some reason, Mark 11:23 was a stumbling block. I took several Bible study classes later and came to some clarity, understanding that Jesus used the word mountain as an example of all the things that seemed too big to handle in our lives, things that often have rough terrain and are steep—not easy to climb or navigate. The really scary stuff. He doesn't want us to be scared.

He wants us to stand boldly in faith and tell our "mountains" to be removed from our lives and cast them into the sea, knowing they are gone forever. That can happen if we have faith that He can do it. I can now say boldly, "I have mountain-moving faith, and I thank You, Lord, that this mountain is removed and cast into the sea!"

CAROL MACKEY

FAITH STEP

Which mountains in your life do you want the Lord to move? Write them down and have faith that He will remove them. When He answers your prayer, write that down too.

THURSDAY, MARCH 7

Jesus said to her, "I am the resurrection and the life. The one who believes in me will live, even though they die; and whoever lives by believing in me will never die. Do you believe this?"

JOHN 11:25–26 (NIV)

WE HAVE A BIBLE STORYBOOK from which we read to our kids every night. Usually Harper stretches out on the couch, and Grace and Adelaide take turns sitting on the floor in front of my chair while I comb out their hair. Stone sits in his chair with his reading glasses on, and Stella perches on his lap so she can see the pictures.

The other night we were reading the story of Jesus's Crucifixion, which the writer handled delicately. It seemed to me to have the right balance of realism along with sensitivity to a child's perspective. So there was the sadness of the death without its being gruesome. We all paused to respect the story and give gravitas to the moment of Jesus's death on the Cross. After a silence, Stella bounced up and down on her daddy's lap. "I love the next page! Turn it, Daddy!"

We all looked at her, questioning.

"It's when Jesus comes alive!"

I want to carry that with me every day for the rest of my life. The simple truth, the excitement, the childlike acceptance of the miracle. The anticipation. The redemption. Most of all, the hope I saw in my daughter's eyes.

The story of Jesus is the greatest story ever told. Because He died and rose again, there is hope for the world.

GWEN FORD FAULKENBERRY

FAITH STEP

During this Lenten season, turn the page in your own life. Let Jesus take you from death into the promise of His Resurrection. Join with Him and commit to living His abundant life today!

FRIDAY, MARCH 8

When the Son of Man returns, how many will he find on the earth who have faith?

LUKE 18:8 (NLT)

I SMILE AT THE LIGHT in my husband's eye as he measures sugar and pours it into the water-filled feeding tube. He gently stirs the mixture until it's the perfect blend. Then he secures the cap and goes outside to hang it on the hook by the window. It's that time of year again, and he is preparing to welcome back the hummingbirds to our deck feeder.

Before I met my husband, I knew the basics of hummers: They're tiny and their wings beat quickly. But nothing in my world had been affected much by their flight patterns, their feeding habits, their personalities or even their beauty.

Now I enjoy watching our tiny friends return each spring almost as much as I enjoy my husband's delight in them. He loves how, when we're picnicking on the deck, they flit close by to let him know their sugar water is all gone. He's fascinated by how one bird assumes the alpha role and chases others from the feeder. There's a lot to hummingbirds, and he never fails to be prepared for them each spring.

Recently he said he likens that preparation to our trust in Jesus' promise to return. It's Easter season now, so those matters are particularly on our minds.

Many people are surprised to see hummingbirds back already. Most people wait to prepare the sugar water until after they see one bird. My husband likes to be ready early, though, and acts in faith that the hummers will return. I love his insights. We have yet to see the first hummer this season, but we are prepared.

I believe God intended His creation to reveal clues to His love for us. I know those special birds will always remind me to keep trusting in Jesus' inevitable second coming.

And I can't help but wonder if my moment-by-moment living reflects a solid faith and preparedness for that day.

ERIN KEELEY MARSHALL

FAITH STEP

What do nature's details reveal about Jesus's love for you? How does your life show you're prepared for His arrival?

SATURDAY, MARCH 9

But the angel said to the women, "Do not be afraid; I know that you are looking for Jesus who was crucified. He is not here; for he has been raised, as he said. Come, see the place where he lay. Then go quickly and tell his disciples, 'He has been raised from the dead.'"

MATTHEW 28:5–7 (NRSVUE)

THE EXPERIENCE THAT MAKES THE GUARDS of Jesus's tomb shake and act like dead men is the same experience that makes these wonderful women rush to declare the impossibly good news: Jesus has been raised!

And just as we all have those parts of ourselves that are like those terrified guards—trying to protect that which is empty and no longer alive in the Spirit—so we all have those parts of ourselves that are like these courageous women. Mary Magdalene had the resources to build the ministry behind Jesus's ministry. She had the courage to stand witness with her friends as they all lost Jesus to His Crucifixion. She had the consciousness to experience the Resurrection and speak joyful truth in a time of fear and despair. Oh, how I want to be with Mary Magdalene this Easter!

There is plenty going on in the world today—and perhaps in your personal life as well—that seems as earth-shattering as the Crucifixion and the earthquake some experienced back then. With dramatic change, sudden loss, and world events we cannot control, can we tap into the Mary Magdalene within each of us? If we can, we will find ourselves experiencing a truly inspired faith. Surrounded by a world steeped in fear, we will also experience true peace, and we will be quick to share news of this peace with others.

ELIZABETH BERNE DeGEAR

FAITH STEP

In your search for Jesus before Easter dawns, spend some time with Mary Magdalene, the first to experience and proclaim the Resurrection. Find inspiration in her vision and courage, so that you, too, may find the heart to share good news, even when all seems dire.

SUNDAY, MARCH 10

We're all like sheep who've wandered off and gotten lost. We've all done our own thing, gone our own way. And God has piled all our sins, everything we've done wrong, on him, on him.

ISAIAH 53:6 (MSG)

It seems safe to say that we don't understand sacrifice as people in biblical times did. Our churches don't smell of blood. We don't hear the cacophony of penned animals in the parking lot. If we think of lambs at all, we picture cute, woolly creatures. They don't carry the connotation of death like they did when John introduced Jesus as the Lamb of God. Anyone listening would have made the connection, especially when John added the descriptor, "who takes away the sin of the world."

God made this sacrifice personal. Every year at Passover good Jews chose a flawless lamb on the tenth day of the month, one for each family. They separated the lamb from the rest of the flock and took special care of it. For most of a week, it was penned and pampered, fed, and watered, often by the children, until the evening of the fourteenth day when each family killed their lamb, smeared its blood on their doorposts, and then roasted and ate it. Little children knew what would happen to the lamb they cared for that week. They grew up knowing that sin required sacrifice.

We need to realize it too. Too often, we act as if we can earn God's mercy. As if through trying harder, we might deserve to be forgiven. We can't. We're broken. We sin. Like sheep, we wander. Robert Farrar Capon said, "The finding, the saving, are all in his hand—the sheep do nothing but get lost. It's all grace."

Jesus, the Lamb of God, the perfect sacrifice, took our sins on Himself. For us. Grace.

SUZANNE DAVENPORT TIETJEN

FAITH STEP

God knows who you are and what you're made of. Accept the fact you're flawed and need a Savior. Today, thank Jesus for loving you just the way you are and coming to be a sacrifice for you.

MONDAY, MARCH 11

Suppose one of you has a hundred sheep and loses one of them. Doesn't he leave the ninety-nine in the open country and go after the lost sheep until he finds it? And when he finds it, he joyfully puts it on his shoulders and goes home. Then he calls his friends and neighbors together and says, "Rejoice with me; I have found my lost sheep."

LUKE 15:4–6 (NIV)

I GET LOST. A LOT. Even when I use my GPS, I often manage to take a wrong turn. My most recent adventure landed me on a dirt logging road blocked by a fallen tree, not quite sure where I went wrong. And as I listened to Madam GPS, her voice sounded the tiniest bit frustrated, as she said, "Recalculating."

There are times I get lost in my personal life as well. Last month, I failed to follow Jesus's directions on loving others, and as a result, I almost allowed a friendship to die from lack of attention. Without meaning to, I'd hurt someone and disappointed the Lord. Like my driving blunders, it wasn't something I'd set out to do. I'd just taken a wrong turn and wound up where I shouldn't have.

The regret I felt was tremendous. But as He carries me back to the fold, I'm certain that whatever sin I've committed, whether accidental or intentional, is forgiven. The moment I repent, He erases it. As I sigh, grateful for the Good Shepherd's patience and love, I imagine His relief in finding me. He's as happy to welcome me back as I am to return to the flock.

The longer I live in faith, the deeper this understanding is driven into my heart. When I walk close beside my Shepherd, I'm less likely to stray and become lost. But those times when I do stray, I'm so glad I can depend on Jesus.

HEIDI GAUL

FAITH STEP

Purchase a Bible and leave it somewhere you think a lost soul might find it. Help the Good Shepherd add another sheep to His flock.

TUESDAY, MARCH 12

He called out to them, "Friends, haven't you any fish?" "No," they answered. He said, "Throw your net on the right side of the boat and you will find some." When they did, they were unable to haul the net in because of the large number of fish.

JOHN 21:5–6 (NIV)

I COUNTED THE NUMBER OF CHILDREN on the list again, and then recounted the number of Bibles, gifts, and stuffed animals. Easter was fast approaching, and we didn't have enough items for the baskets.

My husband and I direct a ministry, Baskets of Joy, that provides Easter baskets to children living in children's homes, foster homes, and shelters. Each basket contains a Bible, a stuffed animal, candy, and several gifts, and is a tangible representation of Jesus's love, so each child feels special and knows someone cares—most of all Jesus.

Each year after Easter, we start preparing for the next year. We purchase Easter sale items and other clearance merchandise, and donations start to flow in. But as I stood over the baskets one Easter season, I started to worry. Despite our best efforts, we were missing lots of items. We needed a miracle.

But then my friend Belinda reminded me that if we trusted Jesus He would provide. So we prayed. The next day we prayed some more. Nothing happened, but we kept on praying. Then one day people started dropping off donations, some by the carload! It reminded me of the disciples and the big haul of fish they caught after trusting Jesus's command to let down their nets.

That year we received so many unexpected donations that we had extra supplies for the following Easter. That was also the year I learned not to worry and to trust Jesus for miraculous provision.

KATIE MINTER JONES

FAITH STEP

Ask Jesus to teach you to trust Him to provide for you.

WEDNESDAY, MARCH 13

By day the Lord commands his steadfast love, and at night his song is with me, a prayer to the God of my life.

PSALM 42:8 (ESV)

Sometimes I am afraid of the dark. I have reason to be. During spring here in the Northwoods, I have been getting home from the hospital in the wee hours of the morning and park at the bottom of the hill that leads to the cabin. April is mud season when snowmelt and frost heave make the driveway impassable.

It's also the time bears emerge from hibernation, feeling more than a little hungry and very protective of their cubs. They aren't looking for a fight, but anyone who inadvertently steps between Mama Bear and her babies is in big trouble. So I sing loudly and shake my keys while I trudge uphill through the mire that, in a month or two, will be my driveway again.

This long-ago Psalmist's emotional state fluctuated from despair to hope like April's thermometer. He longed for God's presence when people jeered, "Where is your God?" He once led worshippers to the house of God with songs and shouts of joy, but now he was cast down and in turmoil. He poured out his heart in prayer as he faced difficulties and dark feelings. He finally counseled himself to hope in the Lord and believe in His love—a love so real that it felt like a presence—the Lord's song with him in the dark.

Jesus still does that. We are not alone. Jesus is with me—with you—whatever we're going through. He said, "Behold, I am with you always (Matthew 28:20, NASB).

He meant it.

SUZANNE DAVENPORT TIETJEN

FAITH STEP

Are you truly alone? Sing a psalm or favorite hymn. Are you feeling alone in a crowd? Try writing a psalm. Whichever you choose, imagine Jesus right there with you in the song.

THURSDAY, MARCH 14

"Even the dogs eat the crumbs that fall from their master's table." Then Jesus said to her, "Woman, you have great faith! Your request is granted." And her daughter was healed at that moment.

MATTHEW 15:27–28 (NIV)

I FEED MY CAT TOMMY on the porch. He considers a half-full bowl unacceptable and scorns it, so I was surprised to find it empty one night. Not a crumb remained. I thought through possibilities—raccoons, skunks, a loose dog? But there was no evidence to support those ideas.

The next evening, I heard strange noises on the porch. I hurried to peek outside.

Surrounding the bowl on skinny stick legs stood a mother bird and her three babies. As they squawked, the mama went from chick to chick, distributing bits of cat food to them. Our bird feeder hung nearby, but this family preferred a seafood mix. Who was I to question? I left them to their meal, but I couldn't stop thinking about them. Were they outcasts in the feathered community?

It reminded me of the Canaanite woman whom Jesus encountered who begged His mercy on her demon-possessed daughter. When she persisted, eager even for a crumb of His healing, He relented.

This winged family bravely dines from the same bowl as their natural enemy. Like them, I've experienced rejection, shame, and the courage born from the will to survive. I've also tasted the sweetness of Jesus's mercy as He meets my needs. He cares for everyone who faces Him in faith and says, "Please, Lord."

Today, I'm hanging another feeder. I want that mama and her babies comfortable and happy. Just like me.

HEIDI GAUL

FAITH STEP

Remember when you've experienced rejection. Have you turned away from someone? Find a way you can help that someone, as the Lord has helped you.

FRIDAY, MARCH 15

You will not have to fight this battle. Take up your positions; stand firm and see the deliverance the LORD will give you, Judah and Jerusalem. Do not be afraid; do not be discouraged. Go out to face them tomorrow, and the LORD will be with you.

2 CHRONICLES 20:17 (NIV)

WHEN A LOVED ONE WAS diagnosed with a serious illness, I jumped into action: appointments with social workers, doctors, palliative care nurses; arranging help; making lists of all the recommendations, medications, and plans from the various specialists. I arranged delivered meals, but my relative didn't like them. I scheduled home care, but she wouldn't allow them to help her clean or cook. Every step felt like a battle. I was running in circles, and nothing was working. My efforts only stressed out my loved one who didn't want help.

At one point, a home care nurse said, "I know you're worried about her, but is it worth fighting all these battles? Even if you do everything right, it won't cure the illness. Perhaps for now it would be wise to focus on other things instead of forcing her to accept help she doesn't want."

The next time I visited, I determined not to drive the agenda, not to scold, not to make suggestions. Instead I listened and validated her feelings and needs. Soon she was sharing childhood stories, and we were laughing together. I was reminded that sometimes I waste energy fighting for control over things that aren't in my control.

There are battles I can't win. Yet Jesus will fight for me. He wins all the ultimate battles. Healing comes—in heaven, if not on earth. Sins are forgiven. Relationships are restored. Not because of my efforts, but because He is with me.

SHARON HINCK

FAITH STEP

Is there a battle He is calling you to relinquish? Stand firm and watch for His salvation.

SATURDAY, MARCH 16

The women hurried away from the tomb, afraid yet filled with joy. . . . Suddenly Jesus met them. "Greetings," he said. They came to him, clasped his feet and worshiped him. Then Jesus said to them, "Do not be afraid . . ."

MATTHEW 28:8–10 (NIV)

MATTHEW TELLS US THAT JESUS's first words after rising from the dead were, "Hello. Do not be afraid." That seems significant to me as a person who tends toward fear. I'm brave only if courage means you do stuff even if you're scared. I do almost everything scared.

I'm not ashamed of being afraid. I think Jesus gives us permission for that in the Garden of Gethsemane, when He's hesitant to go to the Cross. He did it anyway because He knew it was right; it was His purpose, and He was born for it. And He relied on God to give Him strength.

Still, I think we see a different perspective when He has risen from the dead. The women are afraid yet filled with joy. It's as if Jesus wants to give them fullness of joy—to take away their fear so that all that is left is joy. *Greetings. Do not be afraid.*

What must they have felt when they saw Him and heard these words? There must have been tremendous relief when they realized all He said did come true. They watched Him die. They were there as Joseph laid His body to rest. They remembered sitting outside of the tomb and staring at the stone. They hardly dared to hope, but hope they did, and now Jesus stood before them.

First John 4:18 (NIV) says, "Perfect love drives out fear." Because of Jesus, we ultimately have nothing to fear. Death is swallowed up in joy. This is the meaning of Resurrection Day, of Easter—love wins, and joy abounds.

GWEN FORD FAULKENBERRY

FAITH STEP

Plant some seeds in the ground today and wait for them to sprout. Let all of spring remind you that love wins.

SUNDAY, MARCH 17

For just as each of us has one body with many members, and these members do not all have the same function, so in Christ we, though many, form one body, and each member belongs to all the others.

ROMANS 12:4–5 (NIV)

THIS SPRING, MY SIXTH-GRADE Bible class put on a play about the prophet Jonah for our middle school. My friend Alexis was the director. A theater arts major in college, she brought all her gifts to the table: creativity, humor, drama, and fantastic set design. Every student was assigned a part; there were acting roles as well as props, sound, and lighting responsibilities. Weekly rehearsals began with an acting exercise. Even the tech crew and props team had to participate.

Alexis created a sense of purpose and connectedness with the whole class. She said, "You have to be all in. Unless you all give one hundred percent, this play will not work." She was right. If someone missed a cue or forgot his lines, it held everyone else up. Working together, the kids told a funny, poignant, and beautiful story of mercy and forgiveness.

Jesus invites us to tell the same merciful story with our lives. We need to know our part and work together. When we go "off script," embracing our own selfish desires, it affects the whole body of Christ. When we are all in, we forgive those around us. We radiate peace. We lift one another up in moments of joy and share one another's burdens. We are a collective force of love that tells the story of Jesus's grace toward humanity. And that is beautiful.

SUSANNA FOTH AUGHTMON

FAITH STEP

What is your part in telling Jesus's mercy story? Journal your thoughts about what He is asking you to do right now. Thank Him for including you in His great work of love.

MONDAY, MARCH 18

Another angel, who had a golden censer, came and stood at the altar. He was given much incense to offer, with the prayers of all God's people, on the golden altar before the throne. The smoke of the incense, together with the prayers of God's people, went up before God from the angel's hand.

REVELATION 8:3–4 (NIV)

There are many times when I feel like my prayers are useless. I repeat the same thing, day after day, and see no answer from God, no results. Other times, I treat prayer like the least and last thing, when there's nothing else I can do: "I'll pray for you." I say it when I'm feeling helpless and hopeless.

When did prayer become like this for me?

Jesus prayed constantly. He would sometimes stay up all night to pray. He went away to lonely places to pray. He experienced everything we do, so I'm sure there were times He felt like God wasn't hearing Him. In the Garden of

Gethsemane, He prayed for the cup of suffering to pass from Him, and His prayer wasn't answered.

In Revelation, the prayers of God's people are offered with incense on the altar. Our prayers are like incense—an aroma before God, pleasing Him, moving Him. The aroma becomes stronger the more we pray or the more intensely we pray.

Our prayers rise before God's throne. Our prayers reach Him. So even if I feel like my prayers are worthless, or I've become repetitive, I have to remember that they're valuable; they can please God and move Him.

CAMY TANG

FAITH STEP

Is your prayer life stagnant? Give it a new jolt of energy. Remember that your prayers are treasured, that they rise to God where He sits on His throne. Devote yourself to a certain amount of prayer every day this week, and make your prayers incense before God.

TUESDAY, MARCH 19

God, who loved me and gave himself for me.

GALATIANS 2:20 (NIV)

ONE THING I ENJOY ABOUT my little grandson is that he loves to hear me sing. As he grows older, he'll become more discriminating in his musical tastes. I'm sure my voice will lose its charm. But for now, he's happy to hear hymns, standards like "The Wheels on the Bus," and songs that I make up on the spot. This comes in handy when he needs to be soothed or when I'm trying to change the diaper on his squirming bottom.

As I took care of him one week, I added a classic Joe Cocker song to my repertoire; however, I never made it past the first line. "You are so beautiful . . . ." I would sing. Every single time, before I could get out the words "to me," Roman looked up and declared, "I am beautiful." He spoke these words in complete innocence, free of pride, embarrassment, or egotism. Just a simple agreement with my own words.

Roman believes that he's beautiful because his Nana tells him so. He knows he is loved because his family tells him in words and actions. But I couldn't help wondering if Roman's self-esteem will erode as he gets close to the teen years. I remembered my own struggle with a negative self-image, how I let my worth be determined by others' comments or opinions.

Sometimes I have a hard time believing what Jesus says about me. In His eyes, I'm a dearly loved child of God, forgiven, a co-heir to a glorious inheritance. But playing the comparison game can make me feel inferior. And my shortcomings and failures can convince me that I will never measure up. During those moments, I need to remember that Jesus sees me as someone worth dying for. Then I can also say with confidence, "I am beautiful."

DIANNE NEAL MATTHEWS

FAITH STEP

Each time you have a negative thought about yourself today, stop and ask Jesus to remind you how He sees you.

WEDNESDAY, MARCH 20

When Jesus saw his mother there, and the disciple whom he loved standing nearby, he said to her, "Woman, here is your son," and to the disciple, "Here is your mother." From that time on, this disciple took her into his home.

JOHN 19:26–27 (NIV)

Of all the verses that depict Jesus's deep, profound, and tender love for us, this one has always felt the most poignant to me. He was in excruciating pain, beaten, bleeding, hanging on a Cross, bearing the sins of the entire world. Yet as He struggled for breath, He took time to assure the future care of His mother.

When I'm in pain, I rarely muster much interest in those around me. It doesn't take hanging on a cross. To be honest, even a simple headache can make me cranky toward everyone in my path. I don't spare any extra energy to think about their needs. It's all about me.

So the way that Jesus showed care for His mother in this moment when He was fulfilling His purpose on earth seems particularly comforting. His words show me His love, but something else as well. His compassion was eminently practical. He made sure she had a home, someone to provide for her.

There are times when I hesitate to bring my day-to-day concerns to Jesus. Surely with all the huge problems in the world, and in the lives of those I know, He has bigger needs to answer than a broken car, a remodeling project gone awry, or a decision about where to live. But then I remember that at the most painful and crucial moments of His mission on earth, He cared about His mother's welfare and tangible needs. He cares for us as well.

SHARON HINCK

FAITH STEP

Have you ever held back from talking to Jesus about some down-to-earth concerns? Pick three today and ask for His help, knowing He cares.

THURSDAY, MARCH 21

So now there is no condemnation for those who belong to Christ Jesus.

ROMANS 8:1 (NLT)

I'VE ALWAYS HAD A PROBLEM with guilt. As a kid in school, I felt guilty whenever a teacher confronted the class about a problem—even if I had nothing to do with it. When I hear a pastor addressing sinful actions, I want to crawl under the pew even though I may not currently be struggling with what he's discussing. I always imagined that if the doctor slapped my bottom when I was born, I probably tried to say, "I'm sorry. I won't do it again."

Then there are the times when I fail and need to seek forgiveness from my Savior. Even after repenting and confessing my wrongdoing, I have a hard time letting go of the guilt and shame. Instead of putting the mistake behind me and moving on, I get mired down in reliving my failure over and over.

Sometimes I wonder why I struggle so much with guilt and why it's hard to accept the forgiveness that Jesus freely offers. Is it because I'm well aware of what I'm capable of doing? I have no idea where my excessive guilt comes from, but I know where it should go.

Jesus voluntarily offered His life as payment for our sins. His sacrifice took care of all of them—past, present, and future. He died to give us the gift of eternal life, but also so that we can live this earthly life free from guilt and shame. Each time we fail, Jesus stands ready to hear our confession and wash us clean with His forgiveness and mercy. The next time I'm weighed down with guilt, I need to remember to accept His lavish grace.

DIANNE NEAL MATTHEWS

FAITH STEP

Are you struggling with guilt over something that Jesus has already forgiven you for? Read Romans 8 and thank Jesus for the freedom He made possible through His death on the Cross.

FRIDAY, MARCH 22

For God is pleased when, conscious of his will, you patiently endure unjust treatment. For God called you to do good, even if it means suffering, just as Christ suffered for you.

1 PETER 2:19, 21 (NLT)

HAVE YOU EVER BEEN TREATED UNFAIRLY? I had a relationship in which I thought I'd done everything right. I sincerely sought this person's best interests, but I believe that she viewed my actions through the lens of her insecurities and misinterpreted my motives. As a result, she falsely accused me of wrongdoing and cut me out of her life.

How could this happen? Everything inside me screamed to defend myself, and to recite her own wrongdoings. I shed many tears as I prayed for God to open her eyes, change her heart, and maybe teach her a lesson in the process.

In the end, I was the one who learned a lesson. As weeks passed, I reflected on Jesus and the suffering He experienced. He certainly did nothing to deserve false accusations, beatings, and, ultimately, crucifixion. He had every right to defend Himself and point out humankind's flagrant sin against Him. But He remained silent. "He did not retaliate when he was insulted. He left his case in the hands of God, who always judges fairly" (1 Peter 2:23, NLT). What enabled Him to respond in such a way? Knowing that God was His defender.

This truth gave me hope and helped me cope. I chose to follow Jesus's example by trusting God to judge fairly. This meant allowing Him to judge my heart, too, and surrendering this situation's outcome to Him. A huge weight was lifted, and I experienced peace.

Jesus left His case in God's hands. Let's follow in His steps and do the same.

GRACE FOX

FAITH STEP

We're to follow Jesus's example when we suffer unjustly. Are you doing that? If so, great! If not, what changes do you need to make?

SATURDAY, MARCH 23

Jesus said to them, "Have you never read in the Scriptures: 'The stone the builders rejected has become the cornerstone; the Lord has done this, and it is marvelous in our eyes'?"

MATTHEW 21:42 (NIV)

A FRIEND'S FATHER IS A PASTOR, and his congregation built a new church. The architectural design is unique. The building stands on a hill—like a light to the surrounding area. But it was constructed using rough and flawed bricks, symbolic of the imperfect community of believers. In spite of our weaknesses, Christ puts us together to form His Church and to work through us.

What a beautiful reminder that Jesus utilizes us even when the world rejects us. I wish I could be a sturdy, gleaming brick, but I have plenty of cracks and a tendency to crumble under pressure. The strength of Jesus's Church is not in the perfection of each individual, but in the mortar of His grace that holds us together, and in the Cornerstone who is perfect and true and trustworthy.

Jesus understands rejection. He is the foundation of all truth, the corner against which everything else can be measured. Yet He was also rejected. He endured suffering and ridicule, walked the road of death, let His body be broken—all because of His great love for us. Now He invites each of us to be part of His ongoing work on this earth, to fit into His design, to join with other disciples who may also have some rough edges. Together our lives can serve as a temple of worship, a dwelling of shelter for the hurting, and even a home for the lost.

We don't need to be ashamed of our flaws. We can point to the Cornerstone, and trust that Jesus can do His work through the bricks He chooses.

SHARON HINCK

FAITH STEP

Look at some bricks today. Do you spot any cracks or chips? Offer Jesus your life as a brick, trusting that He can build something beautiful.

PALM SUNDAY, MARCH 24

They took palm branches and went out to meet [Jesus], shouting, "Hosanna!" "Blessed is he who comes in the name of the Lord!" "Blessed is the king of Israel!"

JOHN 12:13 (NIV)

In my church on Palm Sunday, or Passion Sunday as it is sometimes called, the children march into the sanctuary singing "Hosanna to the King of Kings" and waving palm branches. It's always a cute spectacle and celebratory in nature. But I find it ironic that it has a much darker meaning.

Passion comes from the word that means "suffer." That we mark Jesus's triumphal entry into Jerusalem as the beginning of His suffering tells us something about the meaning of Palm Sunday. Because while the crowds cheered to welcome Him, they had no idea what He was about.

They hoped He was the Messiah, which to their minds meant a political leader who would overthrow the Romans. This was symbolized by the palms. The focus of the people was the material world—which vastly underestimated Him. Jesus's mission was something far greater. The crowds also showed the fickleness of the human heart. It only took a few days for the cheers to turn to shouts of anger and insult.

The same voices crying "Hosanna!" on this day soon would be calling for Pilate to "Crucify Him!"

As Jesus did, we know where the story is going and we cling to that hope. But even as our eyes are fixed on Easter morning, let us not forget the rough and rocky road He took to get us there.

GWEN FORD FAULKENBERRY

FAITH STEP

Holy Week is a time for reflection. In what ways can you identify with Jesus's experience of being celebrated by the crowd, only to soon be maligned? Is there a time you've praised Him, only to discard Him when He didn't perform what you expected? If you haven't already, ask Him to forgive you for that.

MONDAY, MARCH 25

For I am not ashamed of this Good News about Christ. It is the power of God at work, saving everyone who believes—the Jew first and also the Gentile.

ROMANS 1:16 (NLT)

As I strolled in my parents' yard that late March afternoon, I pulled my heavy sweater tighter to ward off the chilling breeze. It was unusual to have such a cold spring day in west Tennessee. I looked at the gray, leafless trees in the woods across the road. They seemed to doubt that spring had really arrived.

My mother's flower bed, however, told a different story—one that contrasted sharply with the weather and the trees' appearance. The bright yellow daffodils and vivid pink and purple hyacinths rose up from the ground as though they were boldly standing up for some unpopular cause. The more I gazed at those flowers, the more I felt as though they offered a picture of faith, the kind of faith that Jesus wants me to have.

On some days my world seems cold and gray. Circumstances crop up that don't make sense to me. During those times I have to make a choice. Will I look at my situation and give in to doubts? Or will I keep my eyes on Jesus and trust that He has a plan for whatever is happening and He will see me through it?

Then there are times when I'm tempted to blend in with my environment rather than stand out as a follower of Jesus. Do I really want to bow my head and pray as people watch in a crowded restaurant? When someone makes a statement mocking Jesus or the Gospel, do I dare risk speaking up and possibly being labeled a fanatic? It might be easier to keep a low profile, but how can I be ashamed of the One who gave His life for me?

DIANNE NEAL MATTHEWS

FAITH STEP

As you go about your day, ask Jesus to help you watch for opportunities to take a bold stand for your faith rather than blending in with your environment.

TUESDAY, MARCH 26

A man's mind plans his way [as he journeys through life], But the LORD directs his steps and *establishes them.*

PROVERBS 16:9 (AMP)

RECENTLY I HAD TO MAKE a difficult career decision. I wanted to make sure I wasn't stepping out of the will of God by trying to escape an arduous assignment for something easier. I prayed, asking Jesus to make the decision for me. Shortly after praying that prayer, I found out that is not how Jesus operates. The choice was mine. But I wanted to make sure I was making the right choice. I didn't want to be thrown into chaos all over again. I was also comfortable in my current position. Was I afraid to leave my familiar surroundings?

After much prayer, I decided to stay in my current position. Again I sought the guidance of Jesus, asking Him to close the door on the other option if I was making the right decision. But Jesus kept the other door open, and I continued to vacillate between the two choices. I wanted to choose correctly.

Mid-process, I began to realize that I can make plans, but ultimately Jesus is the One who will direct my path if I trust in Him. Regardless of our decisions in some areas of our lives, Jesus will have His way. When we seek His guidance, He will determine the direction of our steps and authenticate our decisions, assuring us that we are on the right course.

After much back and forth, I chose to make the career move. I know I will miss the familiar surroundings, but I am confident that Jesus is directing my steps. Even though I am uncertain about what I will face, I believe it'll be a good career decision. I know that Jesus is leading the way.

TRACY ELDRIDGE

FAITH STEP

When making potentially life-changing decisions, go to Jesus in prayer for guidance. "Lean not on your own understanding; In all your ways acknowledge Him, And He shall direct your paths" (Proverbs 3:5–6, NKJV).

WEDNESDAY, MARCH 27

You were saved by faith in God, who treats us much better than we deserve. This is God's gift to you, and not anything you have done on your own.

EPHESIANS 2:8 (CEV)

If I'm honest, I have to admit I struggle to understand the Cross. We live in a world where, at least in modern countries, there is little concept of blood sacrifice. In ancient times, it was the way things were done. People sinned, then brought sacrifices to atone for their sins. The sins were symbolically placed on the animals, which were then killed for the sins. Gory? Yes, but I'm sure it made sense to ancient people.

The Cross would have made sense to them as well. In fact, it had to be done this way to make sense at all. Jesus was the perfect sacrifice, once and for all, for the sins of the world. I can talk about this all day, but do I really get it? No.

A little Tozer helps illuminate. A. W. Tozer writes, "We please Him most, not by frantically trying to make ourselves good, but by throwing ourselves into His arms with all our imperfections and believing that He understands everything—and still loves us."

I think what the Cross means is that I don't have to be good for Jesus to save me. He already did. I don't have to sacrifice anything, or clean myself up, or atone for the evil things I've done and am. When I try to do those things, not only is it useless, but it takes away from the Cross—it insults what He did. The way I show my appreciation is to run to Him and let myself be loved, with all my imperfections. It's free. I don't get this either. But I'm so thankful.

GWEN FORD FAULKENBERRY

FAITH STEP

Search YouTube for the song that reminds you most of Jesus's love. Close your eyes and listen to it, meditating on the lyrics that speak to your heart.

MAUNDY THURSDAY, MARCH 28

Then he took the cup, gave thanks and offered it to them, saying, "Drink from it, all of you. This is my blood of the covenant, which is poured out for many for the forgiveness of sins."

MATTHEW 26:27–28 (NLT)

Raindrops gray against the windshield; the wipers swoosh, swoosh. As our SUV covers the miles to faraway family, my thoughts travel through time. It's Maundy Thursday. Christendom is mellowed in the holy hush preceding Easter. I haven't known many Good Fridays that weren't rainy, and apparently this year the weather started early.

How appropriate that the sky still cries as the heavens recall the agony approaching the day of the Cross, the day of greatest sorrow. Jesus was about to face physical agony most of us cannot comprehend. Yet His greatest suffering was spiritual because His Father—Almighty, Abba, Yahweh—was about to turn His face away from the sin Jesus would wear. Our sin.

And Maundy Thursday, the day of betrayal, was the last day the disciples would remain ignorant to Jesus's ultimate purpose on earth. The following day all hell would break loose on their friend and mentor. But on this day, what was the atmosphere as they gathered for the Last Supper? I imagine the faces of each disciple, one by one tensing with growing apprehension, sadness. Why was Jesus speaking this way, these mysterious words of betrayal, eating of His body, His blood poured out for forgiveness of sin, His Father's kingdom?

As Jesus spoke to prepare them, He still speaks to us. Sometimes His quiet voice urges us that change is coming. Sometimes He lets us know that rejoicing is soon to come, so hold on. Let your soul mellow in tune with your Savior's. Enter into the holy hush. Consider the grief. But never lose sight of Resurrection day around the corner.

The disciples' greatest loss was soon changed to rejoicing. Yours will be too.

ERIN KEELEY MARSHALL

FAITH STEP

Write a letter to Jesus about whatever comes to mind this Maundy Thursday.

GOOD FRIDAY, MARCH 29

When they were finally tired of mocking him, they took off the robe and put his own clothes on him again. Then they led him away to be crucified.

MATTHEW 27:31 (NLT)

I LOVE THE THOUGHT OF FRESH STARTS and living free because of all Jesus did on the Cross. (Christ is risen! He is risen indeed!) It is easy for me to skim right over the Good Friday part of Easter because it is so very bloody and traumatic. I can't stand the thought of His suffering, the evil of those who set their hearts against Him, and the weeping of a mother seeing her son die.

I want the glory of Sunday morning and the angels and everything being set right. I want to get to the part where the stone is rolled away and the excitement of the empty tomb. The part where the disciples are incredulous when Jesus walks through locked doors and shows up asking for dinner. The truth is that there is no glorious "Christ is risen" without the preamble of "Christ has died."

It is the awfulness of Good Friday that makes Easter so good. It is in His facing and conquering of death that we can see a way out of our own mess. He didn't do it just so it would make a good Bible story. He died so we can get a chance at living the life He designed us for. Of being infused with His Spirit and being more than we ever thought we could be. He died because He loved us. Period.

And how do we, broken people that we are, respond to all that good strong loving? We can stand with hearts open, not sidestepping Good Friday but acknowledging the severity of the Cross, and say, "I know what You did for me and I am thankful." And I am just that. Thankful.

SUSANNA FOTH AUGHTMON

FAITH STEP

Draw a picture of a cross in your journal. Write "Jesus loves me" across the center. Spend some time meditating about all Christ went through to save you and thank Him for it.

HOLY SATURDAY, MARCH 30

Weeping may endure for a night,
but joy comes *in the morning.*

PSALM 30:5 (NKJV)

Waiting. That's what Holy Saturday is about. As Jesus remained in the tomb, I imagine the disciples beaten and with bloodshot eyes, anxious and afraid. Surely they were asking each other, "What do we do now?"

Like the wife who waits for news of her deployed husband. Like a family in the waiting room during surgery. Like the one waiting on a fertility test. The farmer waiting for rain. Or a child waiting for his parents to come home.

We don't like to wait, especially when we're fearful of the outcome. Waiting can be maddening. Especially when God is silent, we may feel abandoned. At the mercy of our circumstances. It's stressful. Fear-inducing. But Holy Saturday is also the seventh day of the week. I'm sure that was no accident. It was on a Saturday that Jesus "rested" in a cave tomb after the Passion.

There's a message here, I believe, for those of us who wait, a message of rest. Even in the grieving, even in the unknown. Even in the questions and the heartache and the pain. Or maybe especially then. Jesus seems to be calling from the tomb: Find your rest. And hope in Me.

GWEN FORD FAULKENBERRY

FAITH STEP

As you observe Holy Saturday, hold fast to this promise: "But those who wait on the LORD shall renew *their* strength; They shall mount up with wings like eagles, They shall run, and not be weary, They shall walk and not faint" (Isaiah 40:31, NKJV).

EASTER SUNDAY, MARCH 31

Praise be to the God and Father of our Lord Jesus Christ! In his great mercy he has given us new birth into a living hope through the resurrection of Jesus Christ from the dead.

1 PETER 1:3 (NIV)

EASTER MARKS CHRISTIANITY'S DEFINING MOMENT: Christ's Resurrection and the promise of eternal life alongside the Father in Heaven, free from sin, suffering, and death. This amazing grace is the cornerstone of the Christian faith and distinguishes it from other faith traditions. Whoever believes in Jesus shall not perish (John 3:16) and is a new creation (2 Corinthians 5:17) who can enjoy freedom (John 8:36) and an abundant life (John 10:10). Here and now.

I confess that the transforming wonder of Easter dims in the face of the mundane and massive challenges of daily life. My wary, intellectual skepticism rears its head. Most days I don't feel newly born, spiritually or otherwise. And, at fifty, death from a terminal illness doesn't seem as remote as it once did. Yet, like so many aspects of our faith, the truth trumps my feelings. The wonder of Easter is renewed by seeking Him in quiet reflection.

Peter captures the wonder so beautifully in just a few words. Indeed, how gracious the mercy of our God to have given us new life this side of Heaven and life eternal with Him through Christ even while we were still sinners (Romans 5:8). That is a hope that transforms us and our experience of this world.

The Gospel of Christ on the Cross proclaims, "I love you enough to give my life so you can have new life, full and free." Resurrection Sunday declares we shall live together in glory forever.

ISABELLA CAMPOLATTARO

FAITH STEP

This Easter, rejoice in the loving, gracious promise of the resurrected Christ. New life and eternal hope. He is risen indeed!

Contributors

Susanna Foth Aughtmon: pages 16–17, 30–31, 72–73, 96–97

Isabella Campolattaro: pages 100–101

Elizabeth Berne DeGear: pages 14–15, 56–57

Tracy Eldridge: pages 90–91

Gwen Ford Faulkenberry: pages 26–27, 52–53, 70–71, 86–87, 92–93, 98–99

Grace Fox: pages 34–35, 44–45, 82–83

Heidi Gaul: pages 42–43, 60–61, 66–67

Lisa Guernsey: pages 5–7

Sharon Hinck: pages 28–29, 38–39, 48–49, 68–69, 78–79, 84–85

Katie Minter Jones: pages 62–63

Rebecca Barlow Jordan: pages 8–9

Keri Wyatt Kent: pages 12–13

Carol Mackey: pages 50–51

Erin Keeley Marshall: pages 54–55, 94–95

Dianne Neal Matthews: pages 18–19, 22–23, 32–33, 40–41, 46–47, 76–77, 80–81, 88–89

Cynthia Ruchti: pages 10–11, 20–21, 24–25, 36–37

Camy Tang: pages 74–75

Suzanne Davenport Tietjen: pages 58–59, 64–65

A Note from the Editors

We hope you enjoyed *Walking with Jesus: Devotions for Lent and Easter*, published by Guideposts. For over 75 years, Guideposts, a nonprofit organization, has been driven by a vision of a world filled with hope. We aspire to be the voice of a trusted friend, a friend who makes you feel more hopeful and connected.

By making a purchase from Guideposts, you join our community in touching millions of lives, inspiring them to believe that all things are possible through faith, hope, and prayer. Your continued support allows us to provide uplifting resources to those in need. Whether through our communities, websites, apps, or publications, we inspire our audiences, bring them together, and comfort, uplift, entertain, and guide them. Visit us at guideposts.org to learn more.

We would love to hear from you. Write us at Guideposts, P.O. Box 5815, Harlan, Iowa 51593 or call us at (800) 932-2145. Did you love *Walking with Jesus: Devotions for Lent and Easter*? Leave a review for this product on guideposts.org/shop. Your feedback helps others in our community find relevant products.

Made in the USA
Monee, IL
14 February 2024

53540832R00066